Anton Stepanovich Arensky

CONCERTO

IN F MINOR

for

PIANO AND ORCHESTRA

OP. 2

MMO 3080

Anton Arensky s Piano Concerto, op. 2

For anyone already acquainted with his iridescent music, mere mention of the elegantly allitera- tive name Anton Arensky instantly evokes the glittering culture of late-nine- teenth-century Russia, of the lost charms of pre-Revolutionary St. Petersburg and Moscow. This was the great Late Romantic period in Russian music, which was initially due in no small part to the influence of Anton Rubinstein, the phenomenally gifted pianist and composer who was instrumental in bring- ing Russia into the forefront of the European musical scene. In the 1860s, Rubinstein and his brother Nikolai respectively founded the music conservatories in St. Petersburg and Moscow, through which subsequent genera- tions of remarkably talented composers were trained. And among the most talented of these students was the pianist and composer Anton Arensky, who always crafted his work with the technical brilliance and compositional sophis- tication that was his acknowledged trade- mark.

Once heard, Arensky's music is as unde- niably attractive to us today as it was a hun- dred years ago—which makes it not always easy to understand why, until recent favor-

able reevaluations, his body of work should have suffered any form of eclipse whatsoever. And Arensky's body of work is considerable: a piano concerto, a fantasia for piano and orchestra, a violin concerto, two symphonies, three operas, a ballet, chamber music, many songs, a huge amount of choral work and vast list of work for his instrument of choice, the piano. All of which he managed to create in less than twenty-five years.

It should not be forgotten that Arensky was an integral element in the fomenting national Russian musical scene of that country's most important musical époque. Arensky's creden- tials were of the highest order. Rimsky-Kor- sakov was his teacher; he was taken under the wing of Tchaikovsky; and among his own intensely appreciative students were Scriabin and Rachmaninov, the latter student so grate- ful to Arensky's guidance that he dedicated several works to him. It was most likely Aren- sky who suggested to the young Rachmaninov that he should tackle, just as he did himself, the composition of a piano concerto while still very young.

And here can be found the probable source of Arensky's temporary eclipse—he literally came to be overshadowed by those very titans he was so close to: his idol Tchaikovsky and his dazzling student Rachmaninov. Nor did it well serve his reputation that his former teacher, Rimsky-Korsakov, nastily diminished Arensky's considerable talent in his memoirs, due most likely to petty jealously on Rimsky-Korsakov's part. These events, as well as an early death before the age of forty-five and an enigmatic personality, helped to cast an undeserved veil over Arensky, who'd been so enormously successful and respected in his lifetime.

The final word about Arensky, however, lies in his music, the bulk of which was never considered less than first-rate by his contemporaries, and which was played for decades after its composition by the world's greatest artists in the very best concert halls. And when played today, Arensky's work surprises one not only by its sparkling vitality but also by its enchanting Russian tone, all the while still remaining thoroughly a part of the European musical tradition.

Anton Stepanovich Arensky was born in Novgorod, Russia, on 12 July 1861, into a relatively affluent family with strong musical leanings. His father was a doctor as well as a keen amateur cellist. As a boy Anton was initially taught the piano by his mother, who herself was an excellent pianist. Musically precocious, by the age of nine he'd already composed some piano pieces and songs. He entered the St. Petersburg Conservatory in 1879 and was taught by Rimsky-Korsakov, who was immediately impressed by the young man's considerable natural talent. He graduated in 1882 and justifiably won a gold medal for the composition of his Piano Concerto, after which he secured the prestigious post of professor of harmony and counterpoint at the Moscow Conservatory.

Arensky's significant, positive contributions to that conservatory as well as to Moscow's musical scene were rewarded in 1894 by his appointment to the nationally important position of Director of the Imperial Chapel in St. Petersburg, replacing Balakirev. Several years later, in 1901, Arensky left that post with a state pension, enabling him to devote himself full-time to composing, conducting and piano performance. He was quite successful for the remainder of his short life, which unfortunately came to an end only five years later in 1906, in a Finish sanitarium, where he was being treated for tuberculosis.

As with so many artists, Arensky's art and life contradicted one another. His compositions might sparkle and shine with their surface brilliance, but his personal life remained mysterious and troubled. In an almost Dostoyevskian manner, Arensky was an alcoholic and a compulsive gambler from an early age. He never married, and although he was very much liked by almost all that knew him, he apparently was extremely introverted. Sadly, he lacked that self-promotional ability which, though often unpleasant, helps a composer to broaden the base of his fame.

In his Piano Concerto, op. 2, Arensky showcases his greatest single gift: his significant talent for creating rich, attractive melody. He composed this work when he was only twenty years old, which is indeed remarkable considering its technical maturity. And most likely due to the composer's youth, the concerto demonstrates Arensky's early, unabashed influence by the nineteenth century's great masters of piano composition—Chopin, Liszt, Grieg, Tchaikovsky and Anton Rubinstein. This helps to explain why, from its first smashing octaves, we somehow feel immediately comfortable and at home with its harmonic and melodic structure. This very eclecticism helps to keep it very much in the great Romantic tradition, though with an overwhelmingly "Russian" feel.

And as with the best works in that tradition, the concerto is chock-full of wonderfully memorable tunes. It is expertly crafted, with the piano part distinctive and clearly laid out—as one would expect from a master student of Rimsky-Korsakov. But where Arensky distinctively breaks with tradition is in the piece's third movement, were he employs a 5/4 time signature. Arensky's friend Tchaikovsky criticized him for this daring rhythm. Interestingly enough, however, ten years later Tchaikovsky would employ the same device in the last movement of his sixth symphony, the *Pathétique*.

The concerto was instantly popular when it was published in 1883, and it was much loved by many of the greatest pianists of the period. Premiered by renowned Liszt student Paul Pabst (whose edition accompanies this MMO version), it was also played repeatedly by Rachmaninov, and was a favorite of the young Vladimir Horowitz.

—*Douglas Scharmann*

PREFACE
TO THE
MUSIC MINUS ONE EDITION

ANTON ARENSKY'S Piano Concerto in F minor, op. 2 was a popular study and performance piece in the late nineteenth and early twentieth centuries. It eventually lost favor due to the overtly sentimental character of its melodic material and its derivative nature. This is a romantic concerto, and during the last fifty years or so, works in this vein that might not classify as masterpieces have been considered unworthy of attention. Hence, the once-popular works of Anton Rubinstein, Edward MacDowell, Alexander Glazunov and a host of other fine composers have lain neglected for half a century.

The young Arensky used the great works of Chopin, Tchaikovsky, Rubinstein and Grieg as models, and it is fun to locate the references. The piece is well constructed, its form carrying the listener along from theme to theme, contrasting lyrical material with brilliant pianistic passagework. The second movement is very Chopinesque, with a few touches of the Grieg thrown in to good effect. It is a pleasure to play and to listen to. There are only a few surprises in the concerto, including the last movement's time signature, which specifies five beats per bar (an Arensky specialty!).

Technically, the Arensky concerto is by no means easy, requiring a pianistic development equal to, or somewhat greater than, the Grieg A-minor concerto. I would suggest it as an alternative to that wonderful, if a bit overplayed, work. It offers the talented young or less experienced player many opportunities to express a wide range of emotions, to grow technically and to encounter many of the problems inherent in concerto performance. It may also give pleasure to the experienced player who is seeking new material. The Arensky Concerto is a great audience piece and would be a welcome and worthy addition to the performance repertoire.

I have made performance suggestions which will be found as footnotes throughout the score.

—*Paul Van Ness*

MMO's edition uses as its basis the second edition of Arensky's concerto, as edited by Paul Pabst (1854–1897), the well-known German pianist who spent much time in Russia and who premiered this concerto.

Concerto
for
Piano and Orchestra

Anton Arensky
op. 2

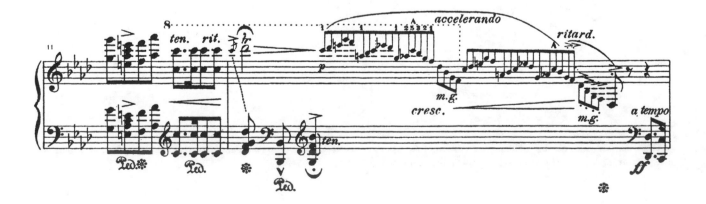

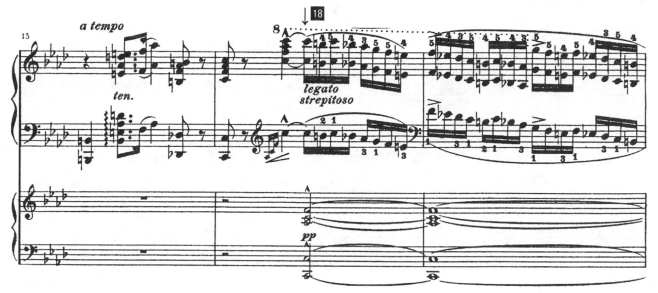

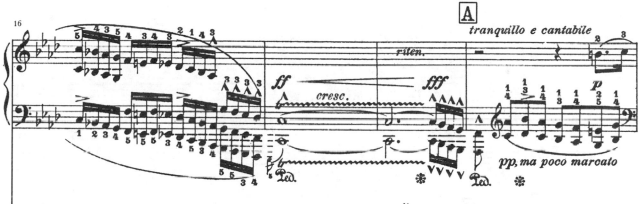

Bar 14: The descending octave passage is to be started quickly, softly and legato. The orchestra should start clearly (^) and the octaves fingered. It is possible to omit the bottom note of the right-hand octaves until bar 16 without losing any of the sweep of the passage (even improving it!) since the crescendo really occurs only at bar 16-17.

Bar 19: the left hand needs to be clear and after the second beat, steady. At bar 22, A controlled ritardando is required and at 23 immediately in tempo.

Bar 27: I use a different fingering than Paul Pabst, the original editor: **12 1234** etc. on the ascending passage in small notes.

Bar 32: Arensky (or Pabst) writes *"avante!"* What he means, I believe, is to play the eighth notes in the first two beats as quasi-16ths, then gradually slow down, *ad libitum* into bar 34. In other words, I hear 32-33 as a very broad single measure, not two!

Bar 39: You could seek out different fingerings from Mr. Pabst's here - it may be easier to play. For the right hand, I use **1** on D, then **2312 4123 1235**, and then come over with the right hand taking the two notes at the downbeat of bar 40 with **4** and **1**. The left hand stays as written.

In the pattern at meaure 43, I use virtually the same fingering as at bar 39: **1 2312 3123 1235** and then over again with the right hand **41**. In the left hand I don't use the **321** etc., I use the same fingering as in bar 39, **5 4212 1** etc. just to keep the pattern going the same way.

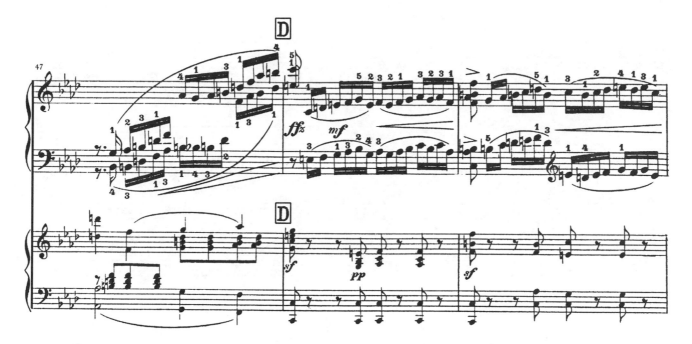

Bar 48: Chopin E minor Concerto! Maintain a steady beat.

14

Bar 56–57: An awkward passage. Practice by omitting the triplet-sextuplet sixteenths. The right hand must remain flexible to move quickly and accurately enough.

Bar 58: The low D on beat 1 is not marked 8va in all editions. I personally prefer not to play the octave.

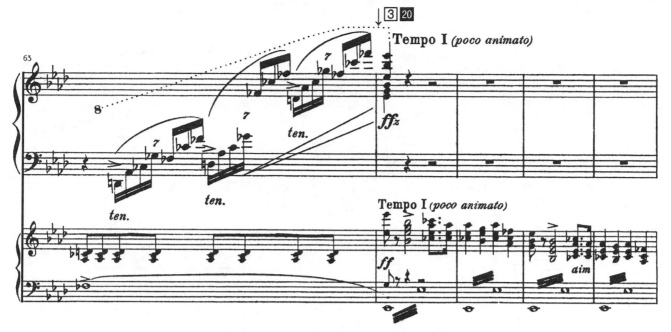

Bar 71: It is important to play this attractive melody simply, with tenderness and color, but without sentimentalizing it.

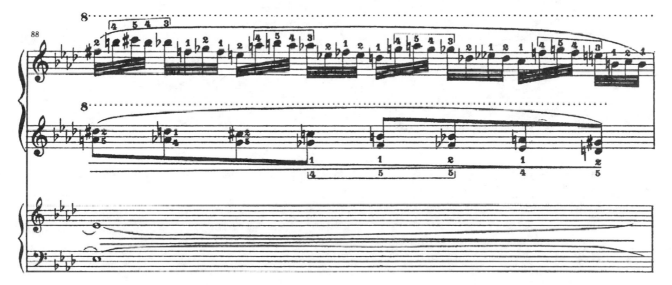

Bars 87-91: Be careful not to rush, and work for a light but clear passage.

Bar 114: I trill the right hand with 2 on E flat and1 on F. This gives a more balanced and brilliant effect for me. The trill must be long and the fermata, a clear silence.

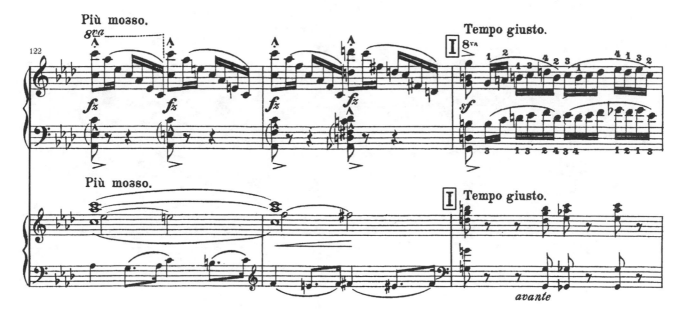

Bars 129-132: A rather difficult passage. The *sforzandi* in 131-32 allow a little time, making them easier than the preceding measures. I slow a little in bar 128 to allow a bit of *"tranquillo"* in 129-30. It is both musically and technically nice!

24

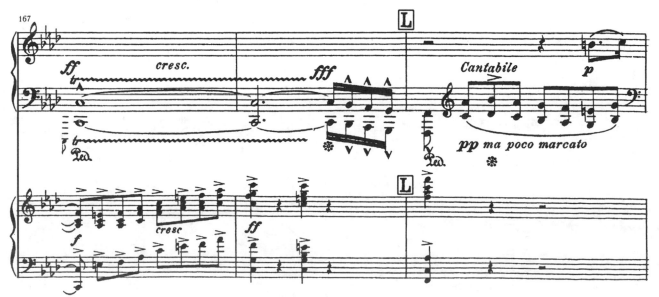

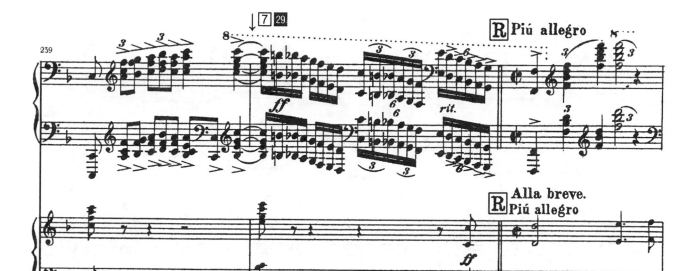

Bar 241-246: does not need to be too fast, but you must be accurate with your leaps! At 247 you are free to start slower and accelerate down at 249. Bring out the rising chordal line powerfully over the orchestra.

II.

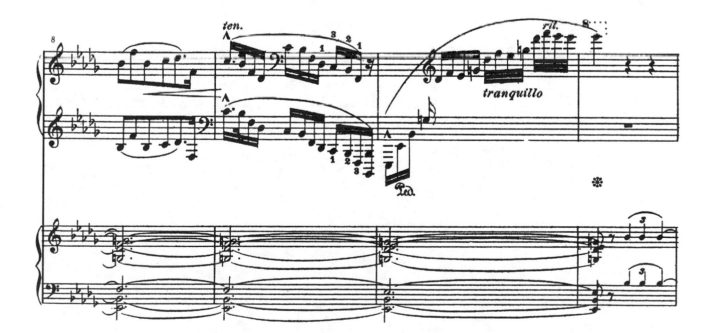

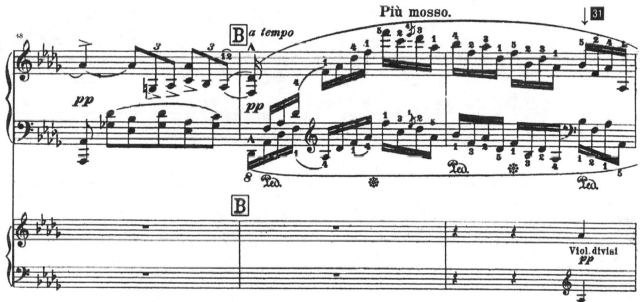

Bars 49-72: All the arpeggio passages must be clearly understood metrically or you will lose sync with the orchestra. It is possible to feel the downbeats in the wrong places! Play as *legato*, delicate and smoothly as possible. At 69-70, the *rubato* will allow the beat to be ambiguous without problem.

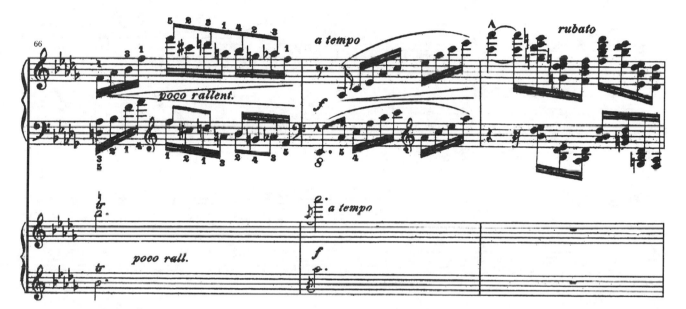

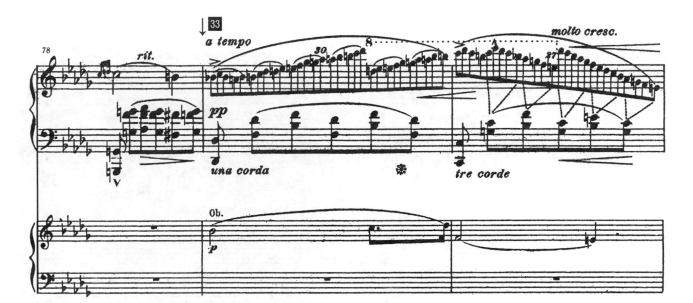

Bars 75-91: Notice the left hand's imitation of the right hand theme. Pretty nice writing for a student composer! The passage at 79-80 isn't really hard and sounds very effective! Play really softly until the descent!

Bar 117: You must be together with the orchestra on the last three eighth notes of this measure and at bar 122. Listen to the violin at 124.

In the orchestral score, the final chord of D-flat major is written as a quarter note with fermata in the orchestra and as a half note with fermata for the final D-flat octave in the piano. I decided to follow that (as does Stephen Coombs in his wonderful Hyperion recording). Of course, it could just be a misprint, so think it over and decide what you like!

III.
Scherzo – finale.

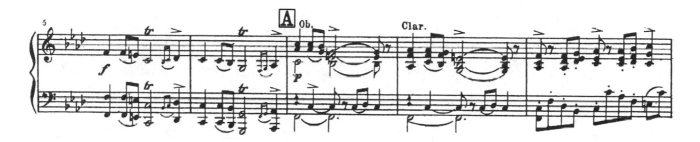

It is tempting to start this movement at a really sizzling speed, e.g. quarter=176. Be careful! There are some passages that won't take that tempo easily! I would opt for a flexible quarter=160.

Bars 19-22: At a tempo that has the requisite scherzo quality, these scales really rip! It's possible to help oneself a little by anticipating the downbeat in the right hand by a few notes, beginning the downward scale about a half-beat early in the right hand, while maintaining the beat in the left.

Bars 23-24: Be aware of the accents and relationship to the orchestra.

49

Bar 52: The tempo slows here and the subsequent solo part should be both dolce and dance-like until-

MMO 3080

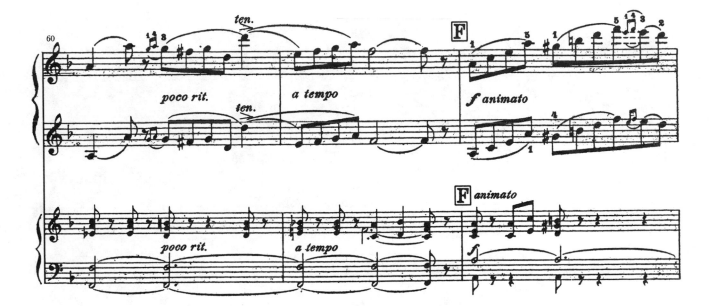

Bar 62-72 *animato!*

Bar 72 resumes the *tempo tranquillo*.

MMO 3080

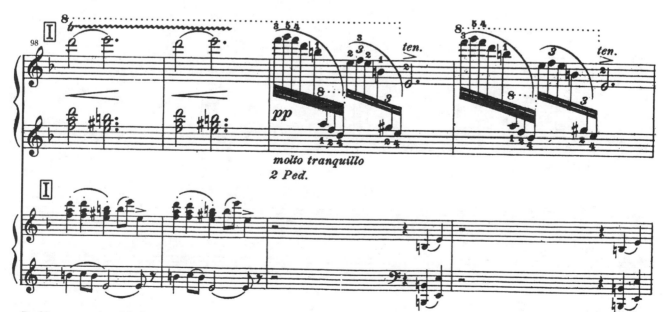

Bar 90 returns to the original tempo.

Bars 100–120: I believe that this passage should be played noticeably slower than a tempo. It is marked *molto tranquillo*. It is possible to rearrange the thirty-second notes between the hands to ease the difficulty in gaining smoothness.

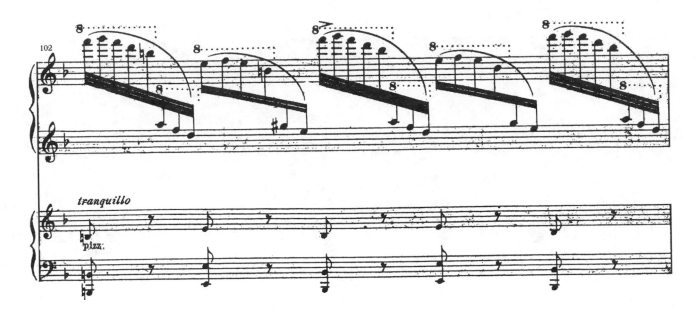

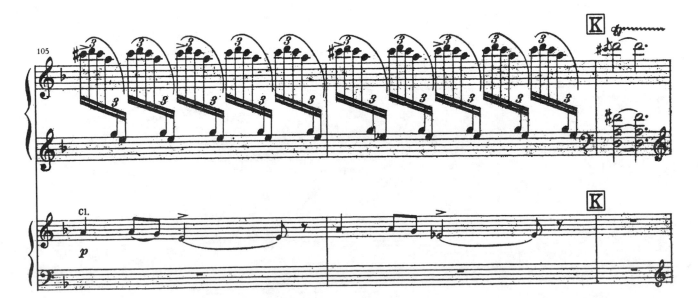

Bar 107: It is interesting to me that the Russian edition omits bar 107 found in the other editions (Rehearsal K) even though the editor is still Pabst. I do not know if this is simply an error, but, in fact, I prefer to omit this measure and would ask to do so in performance. In my opinion, it stops the flow of the music and sounds pedantic, i.e. like a composition teacher said, "Anton, you must resolve to D major before going on."

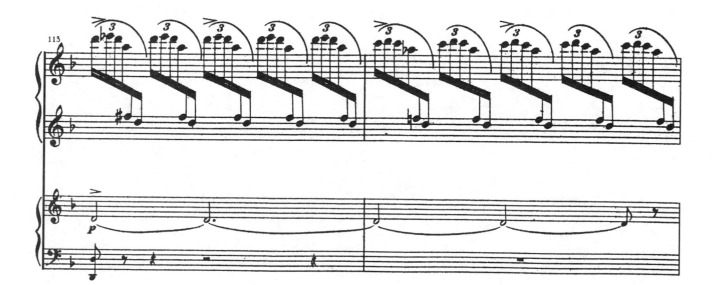

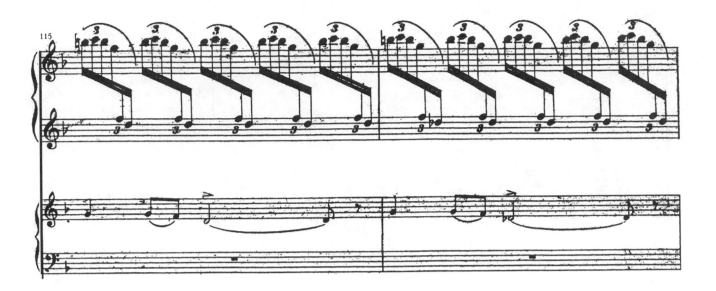

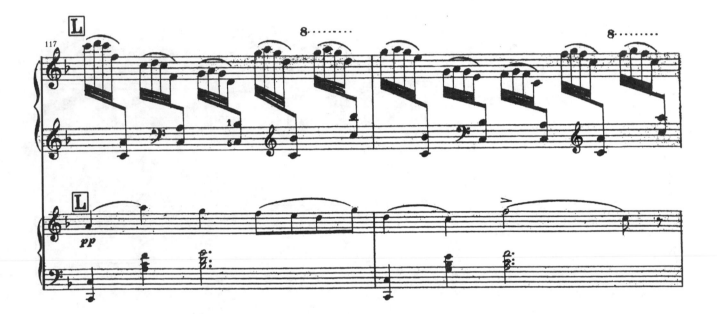

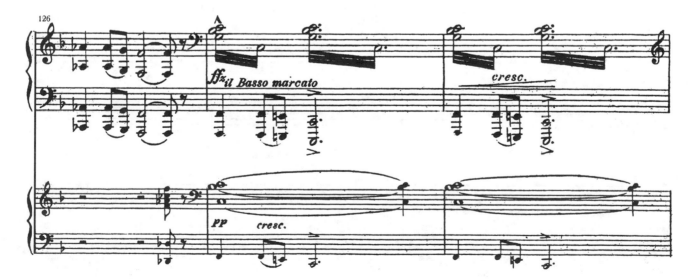

Bar 121-125: This is a perfect place not only to *crescendo* but also to *accelerando* back to Mm 160.

Bar 133: a little air pause before the *subito* *pp* is nice and then watch out for unsteadiness in the beat. Ensemble must be perfect!

MMO 3080

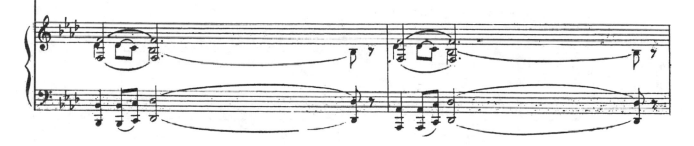

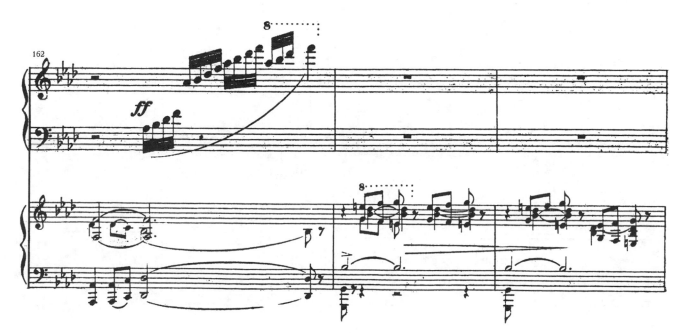

Bar 193-234: Work to be in complete control of the beat and not over-do the *accelerando* to a too fast *presto*. Sweep with beat!

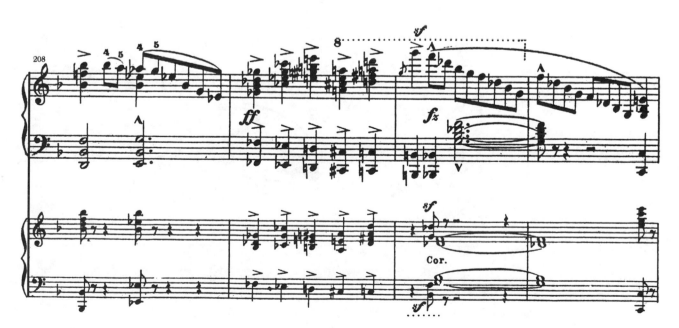

Bars 206–207 may be broadened a bit for clarity.

CLASSICAL PIANO RELEASES

Anton ARENSKY (1861-1906)

PIANO CONCERTO IN F MINOR, OP. 2   MMO CD 3080
Paul Van Ness – Plovdiv Philharmonic Orchestra/Todorov
Anton Arensky, contemporary and friend of Tchaikovsky and Rimsky-Korsakov and teacher of Rachmaninov and Glazunov, composed this vibrant concerto with its lyrical melodies, heroic solo part, and thunderous orchestration, a bravura piece in the great Russian romantic tradition, and technically accessible to the advanced student, making a beautiful alternative to the Grieg concerto for advancing players.

FANTASIA ON RUSSIAN FOLKSONGS, OP. 48   MMO CD 3086
(w/Rimsky Korsakov: Piano Concerto in C-sharp minor)
Victor Tchutchkov – Plovdiv Philharmonic Orchestra/Todorov
Russian master Anton Arensky wrote this exciting fantasia on two Russian folksongs, sounding for all the world like a latter-day movie score, with bravura piano solo integrated. Affording the soloist an opportunity to play an exhilarating piece with a thrilling Russian feel, and at the same time of a manageable length. This little-known piece is highly recommended.

Carl Philipp Emanuel BACH (1714-1788)

CONCERTO IN A MINOR   MMO CD 3059
Neill Eisenstein - Stuttgart Festival Orchestra/Kahn   CASS 331
Carl Philipp Emanuel Bach, a very talented and important proponent of the concerto form, wrote this appealing work in 1750. Filled with expressiveness, it is a fascinating and beautiful representation of the northern German baroque concerto.

Johann Christian BACH (1735-1782)

CONCERTO IN B-FLAT MAJOR, OP. 13, NO. 4   MMO CD 3056
(w/Handel: Concerto Grosso in D, op. 3, no. 6   CASS 347
& Haydn: Concertino in C major)
Neill Eisenstein - Stuttgart Festival Orchestra/Kahn
Johann Christian Bach was the youngest of the Bach sons and Mozart was overwhelmingly influenced by his compositions. This short concerto demonstrates his compositional brilliance. A perfect student concerto.

CONCERTO IN E-FLAT MAJOR, OP. 7, NO. 5   MMO CD 3021
(w/J. S. Bach: Concerto in F minor)   CASS 346
David Syme – Stuttgart Symphony Orchestra/Kahn
Johann Christian Bach, youngest son of J. S. Bach, was a prolific and skillful composer, as this marvelous gem will testify. It is perfect for the beginning student, a wonderful preparation for the Mozart concerti.

Johann Sebastian BACH (1685-1750)

"TRIPLE" CONCERTO IN A MINOR, S1044   MMO CD 3057
(w/Brandenburg Concerto No. 5, 1ˢᵗ movement)   CASS 357
Neill Eisenstein - Stuttgart Festival Orchestra/Kahn
This intricate concerto for keyboard, violin and flute is a challenge, containing much brilliant passagework. The less formidable slow movement was taken from the organ sonata No. 3. It is a companion to the Brandenburg Concerto No. 5, the first movement of which is included on this album. An extremely rewarding and enjoyable piece for study.

Johann Sebastian BACH (cont'd)

BRANDENBURG CONCERTO NO. 5 IN D MAJOR, S1050
   MMO CD 3054
Neill Eisenstein - Stuttgart Festival Orchestra/Kahn   CASS 331
The Brandenburg Concerto No. 5, written for harpsichord, flute, violin and orchestra, was Bach's first truly original keyboard concerto and is a unique work full of bravura passages. An eternal favorite!

CONCERTO IN D MINOR, S1052   MMO CD 3022
David Syme – Stuttgart Symphony Orchestra/Kahn   CASS 317
Bach's beautiful and noble D-minor concerto is a testament to this master's abilities at the keyboard. It is actually a transcription of one of his violin concerti, and Bach has given it a grand treatment, and the expressive slow movement is reminiscent of his famous Italian Concerto. A lovely and rewarding piece.

CONCERTO IN F MINOR, S1056   MMO CD 3021
(w/ J. C. Bach: Concerto in E-flat major)   CASS 346
David Syme - Stuttgart Symphony Orchestra/Kahn
Johann Sebastian Bach's spirited F-minor concerto is wonderfully compact, of a manageable length for the student player, and displaying all the wonderful qualities associated with the granddaddy of the keyboard. Great fun to learn and play!

CONCERTO FOR TWO PIANOS IN C MAJOR, S1061   MMO CD 3055
(w/Schumann: Andante & Variations for Two Pianos,   CASS 332
'Celli and Horn)
Neill Eisenstein – Stuttgart Festival Orchestra/Kahn
This excellent work relies heavily on the two pianos for effect, with a lovely but subdued string accompaniment. Bach dispenses with the strings altogether in the lovely central movement, then ends with an exhilarating fugue. A gem!

Ludwig van BEETHOVEN (1770-1827)

CONCERTO NO. 1 IN C MAJOR, OP. 15   MMO CD 3001
David Syme – Stuttgart Symphony Orchestra/Kahn   CASS 314
The spirited and graceful Concerto No. 1 in C was actually written after the B-flat No. 2. It is an impressive work, filled with wonderful pianism.

CONCERTO NO. 2 IN B-FLAT MAJOR, OP. 19   MMO CD 3002
David Syme – Stuttgart Symphony Orchestra/Kahn   CASS 316
Though published later, the Concerto No. 2 was actually the first of Beethoven's concerti to be written and displays an almost Mozartian style and a solo part that is exciting and beautiful but accessible to less advanced players.

CONCERTO NO. 3 IN C MINOR, OP. 37   MMO CD 3003
David Syme – Stuttgart Symphony Orchestra/Kahn   CASS 315
Little need be said about this wonderful concerto, which shows Beethoven in thorough command of the idiom. Striking passages, its trademark opening theme in octaves, and a marvelous orchestration create an indispensable part of every pianist's library.

CONCERTO NO. 4 IN G MAJOR, OP. 58   MMO CD 3004
Kevin Class – Stuttgart Symphony Orchestra/Kahn   CASS 336
A groundbreaking concerto, introspective yet lofty—universally revered by every great pianist. This is without question one of the greatest concerti ever written.

CONCERTO NO. 5 IN E-FLAT MAJOR,   MMO CD 3005
OP. 73, 'EMPEROR'   CASS 334
Kevin Class – Stuttgart Symphony Orchestra/Kahn
This ever-popular and majestic concerto has never been able to shake off the designation which was given it by a publisher years after its composition. A timeless favorite, filled with striking pianism and orchestration—Beethoven at his most mighty!

Johannes BRAHMS (1833-1897)

CONCERTO NO. 1 IN D MINOR, OP. 15 (2CD set) MMO CD 3009
David Syme – Stuttgart Symphony Orchestra/Kahn CASS 344
This mammoth work is a magnificent concerto cast in the composer's trademark Olympian manner—broad melodic lines, a mixture of German classicism and romanticism as only Brahms could do it. Universally admired as one of the all-time great Romantic concerti.

Fryderyk CHOPIN (1810-1849)

CONCERTO IN E MINOR, OP. 11 MMO CD 3010
David Syme – Stuttgart Symphony Orchestra/Kahn CASS 343
This romantic concerto is one of the composer's few works with orchestra and displays great lyricism and grandeur. Revealing Chopin's unique understanding of the piano, it is a challenging and rewarding work which combines poetry and excitement as only this master could. A high point in the literature, essential for every serious pianist.

CONCERTO IN F MINOR, OP. 21 MMO CD 3075
Raluca Stirbat – Plovdiv Philharmonic Orchestra/Todorov
Chopin's most magnificent piano concerto is now available from MMO. Chopin's F-minor concerto is a remarkable composition, filled with soaring passages and a heart-melting *Larghetto* of unmatched lyricism. A masterpiece which holds a very special place in Chopin's *oeuvre*, and in the entire concerto repertoire.

César FRANCK (1822-1890)

VARIATIONS SYMPHONIQUES MMO CD 3058
(w/Mendelssohn: Capriccio Brilliant) CASS 327
Neill Eisenstein - Stuttgart Symphony Orchestra/Kahn
This famous shorter concerted piece is a single movement of variations, gorgeously composed in Cesar Franck's inimitable style. One of the most understated, magnificent works in the Romantic repertoire, a joy for any pianist.

George GERSHWIN (1898-1937)

RHAPSODY IN BLUE MMO CD 3083
Gershwin's masterpiece is now available in a thrilling MMO version! The piano concerto which transformed modern music and integrated jazz sensibilities into "serious" music is a magical experience for player and listener alike.

Alexander GLAZUNOV (1865-1936)

PIANO CONCERTO NO. 1 IN F MINOR, OP. 92 MMO CD 3078
Alexander Glazunov's first concerto is a beautiful piece uniquely constructed in two-movement form, the second movement being a series of variations. Beautiful and perfect writing for the instrument, lush orchestration, a masterwork in the Russian concerto literature.

Edvard GRIEG (1843-1907)

CONCERTO IN A MINOR, OP. 16 MMO CD 3006
David Syme – Stuttgart Symphony Orchestra/Kahn CASS 312
One of the most enchanting and popular piano concerti ever written, this is for many the epitome of nineteenth-century Romanticism, showing the great influence of both Schumann and Liszt as well as Grieg's own fascination with Norwegian folk melodies. One of the most popular offerings in the MMO catalogue, it is less demanding and more accessible to the serious student.

George Frederic HANDEL (1685-1759)

Concerto Grosso No. 5 in D major, op. 3, no. 6 MMO CD 3056
(w/J.C. Bach Concerto in B-flat major CASS 347
& Haydn: Concertino in C major)
Neill Eisenstein - Stuttgart Festival Orchestra/Kahn
Handel's *concerti grossi* are considered the epitome of the baroque concerto form. And this lively example is no exception. A delight!

Franz Josef HAYDN (1732-1809)

CONCERTO IN D MAJOR, HOB. XVIII/10 MMO CD 3023
David Syme – Stuttgart Symphony Orchestra/Kahn CASS 311
This charming piece is Haydn's best-known piano concerto, and is perfect for students, being of only moderate difficulty. It is a consistent favorite, one of the most popular in the MMO catalogue. A delightful work!

CONCERTINO IN C MAJOR, HOB. XIV/3 MMO CD 3056
(w/J.C. Bach Concerto in B-flat major CASS 347
& Handel: Concerto Grosso in D major, op. 3, no. 6)
Neill Eisenstein -- Stuttgart Festival Orchestra/Kahn
Cast in three short movements, this charming little concerto is classic Haydn and is highly enjoyable to play.

Franz LISZT (1811-1886)

HUNGARIAN FANTASIA, S123 MMO CD 3020
(w/Liszt: Concerto No. 2) CASS 345
Neill Eisenstein - Stuttgart Symphony Orchestra/Kahn
Liszt used his own Hungarian Rhapsody No. 14 as the basis for the Hungarian Fantasia. With its triumphal themes, sparkling cadenzas, and breathtaking finale, this single-movement mini-concerto is a sparkling musical gem!

PIANO CONCERTO NO. 1 IN E-FLAT MAJOR, S124 MMO CD 3019
(w/Weber: Konzertstück) CASS 303
Neill Eisenstein - Stuttgart Symphony Orchestra/Kahn
One of the world's all-time favorite piano concerti is a stunning experience for player and audience alike — from the opening octaves through its lush *andante* and its thrilling *marziale* finale—this concerto changed the face of concerto music forever.

PIANO CONCERTO NO. 2 IN A MAJOR, S125 MMO CD 3020
(w/Liszt: Hungarian Fantasia) CASS 345
Neill Eisenstein - Stuttgart Symphony Orchestra/Kahn
Liszt transformed the whole concept of the concerto when he cast this piece in one single movement using the idea of thematic transformation. A poetical masterpiece, both serene and glitteringly exciting, which stands at the very pinnacle of Romantic piano literature.

TOTENTANZ, S126 & S126i MMO CD 3088
(1st "De Profundis" version & standard version)
MMO presents the ultimate Totentanz. Here are both the standard audience-pleaser heard regularly in concert-halls around the world and the sought-after, very different 1849/1853 version with its magnificent, heavenly "De Profundis" section as published in 1919 by Busoni. This MMO edition even includes the alternate variation No. 7, so you can choose the Totentanz you want to perform! This is Liszt at his most spectacular and diabolical—a vital part of every virtuoso's library!

Felix MENDELSSOHN (1809-1847)

CAPRICCIO BRILLIANT, OP. 22 MMO CD 3058
(w/ Franck: Variations Symphoniques) CASS 327
Neill Eisenstein - Stuttgart Symphony Orchestra/Kahn
Mendelssohn's sparkling capriccio brilliant is an enduring favorite, long admired for its compact form and masterful writing. A playful romp!

PIANO CONCERTO NO. 1 IN G MINOR, OP. 25 MMO CD 3011
David Syme – Stuttgart Symphony Orchestra/Kahn CASS 324
Felix Mendelssohn's famous G-minor concerto is a showpiece which demonstrates the composer's pianistic brilliance. One of the most well-known concerti of the early Romantic period..

Moritz MOSZKOWSKI (1854-1925)

PIANO CONCERTO IN E MAJOR, OP. 59 MMO CD 3077
Moritz Moszkowski, the Polish-born composer who settled in Paris and whose music was a favorite of such virtuosi as Vladimir Horowitz, composed this gorgeous concerto in 1898. With its elegant construction, beautiful, luminescent melodies, perfect pianism and masterful orchestration, it is a highlight of the late Romantic Era. This work holds a unique place in the literature, making a rewarding project for any serious pianist.

Wolfgang Amadeus MOZART (1756-1791)

CONCERTO NO. 9 IN E-FLAT MINOR, KV271　MMO CD 3012
David Syme – Stuttgart Symphony Orchestra/Kahn　CASS 328
One of Mozart's greatest concerti, grand and daring for its time, brilliantly written for the soloist. A masterpiece!

CONCERTO NO. 12 IN A MAJOR, KV414　MMO CD 3013
David Syme – Stuttgart Symphony Orchestra/Kahn　CASS 351
This concerto was one of Mozart's personal favorites, and had a great deal of personal meaning to him, as it was written in tribute to his friend and inspiration Johann Christian Bach. The haunting *andante* is based on one of the youngest Bach's themes. Inventive and much fun to play.

CONCERTO NO. 14 IN E-FLAT MAJOR, KV449　MMO CD 3073
Bruce Levy – Plovdiv Chamber Orchestra/Todorov
This inspired concerto is a strikingly original work, combining beautiful melody and a capricious third movement that was very ahead of its time. A charming, delightful work to be enjoyed by pianists everywhere!

CONCERTO NO. 17 IN G MAJOR, KV453　MMO CD 3085
(NEW EDITION)
Paul Van Ness – Plovdiv Philharmonic Orchestra/Todorov
A beautiful Mozart concerto which is particularly notable for the unusually serene character of its first two movements, advanced orchestration and a witty and theatrical final movement. One of Mozart's most distinguished concerti and not too technically demanding.

CONCERTO NO. 19 IN F MAJOR, KV 459　MMO CD 3081
A well-liked Mozart concerto brimming with melody, integrating soloist and orchestra in an almost chamber-music manner. The theme-and-variations *Andante* movement is particularly wonderful. Popular and deservedly so.

CONCERTO NO. 20 IN D MINOR, KV 466　MMO CD 3014
Kevin Class – Stuttgart Symphony Orchestra/Kahn　CASS 308
This concerto, one of only two Mozart wrote in a minor key, is by far the most famous of all his piano concerti and is filled with profound music of the highest order as well as lively and charming themes. Among its later, most ardent admirers were Beethoven and Brahms. Demands sensitivity from the soloist, and is an important work for every pianist to study and learn.

CONCERTO NO. 21 IN C MAJOR, KV467,　MMO CD 3072
"ELVIRA MADIGAN"
Sabri Tulug Tirpan – Vidin Philharmonic Orchestra/Todorov
This justifiably famous piano concerto, with its gorgeous *Andante* theme, became a popular hit when it was used in the film *Elvira Madigan*. Lush melodies orchestrated in Mozart's inimitable style—graceful and elegant pianism throughout. The Classical piano concerto at its height!

CONCERTO NO. 23 IN A MAJOR, KV 488　MMO CD 3015
David Syme – Stuttgart Symphony Orchestra/Kahn　CASS 323
A lovely, popular concerto full of melody and gorgeous orchestration, especially notable for its beautiful use of woodwinds to complement the piano.

CONCERTO NO. 24 IN C MINOR, KV 491　MMO CD 3016
David Syme – Stuttgart Symphony Orchestra/Kahn　CASS 335
Brilliantly written for the instrument, this C-minor concerto is unusual when compared to most other Mozart concerti. A passionate work filled with originality, Mozart employs his largest orchestra, utilizing woodwinds extensively, giving a beautiful effect. Highly recommended.

CONCERTO NO. 26 IN D MAJOR, KV 537,　MMO CD 3017
"CORONATION"　CASS 309
Kevin Class – Stuttgart Symphony Orchestra/Kahn
A delightful, happy concerto which was written for the coronation for Leopold II in 1790 and performed by Mozart at that occasion in Frankfurt. A lovely atmosphere pervades the work, which is tremendous fun to learn.

CONCERTO NO. 27 IN B-FLAT MAJOR, KV595　MMO CD 3082
Bruce Levy – Plovdiv Philharmonic Orchestra/Todorov
Composed in his last year, this subtle and delicate concerto was Mozart's final contribution to the piano concerto literature, and it shows the restraint and precision of a supreme master. A feeling of serenity pervades the entire piece. A joy to perform.

Sergei RACHMANINOV (1873-1943)

CONCERTO NO. 1 IN F-SHARP MINOR, OP. 1　MMO CD 3089
(FIRST VERSION)
Not many people know that the commonly heard version of this great concerto is actually a revision made by Rachmaninov thirty years after composing the original in 1891. The first version, very similar overall to the 1919 version, is technically much less demanding than its successor and is therefore a perfect opportunity for the less advanced pianist or student to play a famous Rachmaninov concerto. MMO is proud to offer this beautiful first version in a world premiere recording.

CONCERTO NO. 2 IN C MINOR, OP. 18　MMO CD 3007
David Syme – Stuttgart Symphony Orchestra/Kahn　CASS 333
Equally renowned as composer and pianist, Rachmaninov dazzled the world with his piano concerto in C minor. It is immensely popular to this day. Brilliant and powerful with the beautiful lyric theme that became the popular song *Full Moon and Empty Arms*, it is here presented in a lovely recording, sans your part, the solo piano.

CONCERTO NO. 3 IN D MINOR, OP. 30　(2CD SET) MMO CD 3074
Alexander Raytchev – Plovdiv Philharmonic/Todorov
Rachmaninov's masterpiece, his largest and most architecturally satisfying piano concerto, became a sensation again in 1996 when it was featured in the movie *Shine*. With its memorable theme and glittering orchestration, for many pianists this is the pinnacle of achievement in the concerto repertoire. MMO's version of this complex and rewarding work is an invaluable and essential asset for every virtuoso-in-training!

RHAPSODY ON A THEME OF PAGANINI　MMO CD 3084
Composed in 1934, this series of variations on one of Paganini's themes was an instant hit. The 18th variation is a universally known melody to this day, being heard on film and television soundtracks, in recordings, and in concert halls everywhere. A bridge between late 19th-century music and the modern age, it is a vital addition to every serious pianist's repertoire.

Nikolai RIMSKY-KORSAKOV (1844-1908)

CONCERTO IN C-SHARP MINOR　MMO CD 3086
(w/Arensky: Fantasia on Russian Folksongs)
Victor Tchutchkov – Plovdiv Philharmonic/Todorov
A good choice for students due to its thoughtfully-written solo part and its short length, this concerto is a Lisztian set of variations on a Russian folk theme, masterfully orchestrated and full of rich pianism in the best Russian Late Romantic tradition.

Anton RUBINSTEIN (1829-1894)

CONCERTO NO. 4 IN D MINOR, OP. 70　MMO CD 3079
Anton Rubinstein's famous "thunder and lightning" concerto of the 19th century, long neglected in late-20th-century concert halls, is now available in a stupendous MMO edition, allowing a new generation of pianists to discover its thrilling octave passages, long, lyrical melodic lines, and beautiful orchestration. It became synonymous with the idea of the heroic concerto in the late 19th and early 20th centuries. This one is a guaranteed crowd-pleaser, and a favorite of every aspiring virtuoso who discovers its power.

Robert SCHUMANN (1810-1856)

CONCERTO IN A MINOR, OP. 54　MMO CD 3008
Kevin Class – Stuttgart Symphony Orchestra/Kahn　CASS 326
The Schumann concerto is felt by many pianists to be the greatest piano concerto ever written. Integrating the piano and orchestra in an unprecedented manner, it embodies the melodic grace and fine tonal texture so characteristic of one of the great composers of all time.

Piotr Ilyich TCHAIKOVSKY (1840-1893)

CONCERTO NO. 1 IN B-FLAT MINOR, OP. 23　MMO CD 3026
David Syme – Stuttgart Symphony Orchestra/Kahn　CASS 300
This staggeringly famous romantic concerto is world-loved and has been a staple since its introduction. Should be in every pianist's repertoire. The quintessential virtuoso concerto!